YOU CAN MAKE A DIFFERENCE

A GUIDE TO BEING A GREAT CONSULTANT

Wendy,

You already make
a difference in our society

Best of Luck.

Zena

Nov. 2023

ZENA SIMCES

You Can Make a Difference
A Guide To Being A Great Consultant
Copyright © 2020 by Zena Simces

Tellwell Talent
www.tellwell.ca

ISBN
978-0-2288-4381-8 (Paperback)
978-0-2288-4380-1 (eBook)

TABLE OF CONTENTS

DEDICATION

I want to thank my husband, Dr. Simon W. Rabkin,
for his patience and helpful suggestions.

Thank you to my wonderful daughters, Simone and Michelle
Vigod, for their unwavering support and thoughtful advice.

FOREWORD

After many years of consulting, I was faced with a project that involved three different organizations as my clients. I thought about all the things a good consultant might do, like getting these clients to agree to a common vision, identifying results they want to achieve, clarifying actions they can undertake, and assisting them to work as a team to reach their goals. As a consultant, you may be familiar with this type of situation.

I did my due diligence on each organization and felt I had a thorough understanding of where these groups were coming from, what they were already doing and what they indicated, on paper, they wanted to achieve. I compiled many good ideas and techniques to stimulate discussion and get the process rolling before I called a meeting.

The first session was a disaster! Each of the organizations did not understand what the other group had accomplished or what they were planning. Everyone talked at cross purposes as the meeting progressed. While they had agreed to a common purpose on paper, in reality, there did not appear to be a common goal. In fact, there were many goals they wanted to achieve. To complicate the situation, when new information was presented to them, they kept changing their minds. I ended up devoting a great deal more time and effort to this project than I had anticipated.

Where did I go wrong?

I must admit, I did not have a good understanding of the personalities of the players involved nor did I thoroughly understand the culture of each organization. It may have saved a great deal of time and heartache to work with each of the groups separately to gain an understanding of their needs, values and perspectives, and to establish a trusting relationship with each prior to bringing them together. Spending time helping the organizations better understand each other's values, goals and programs while building a relationship between them in advance would also have been beneficial.

While I have learned much from my successes, "failures" like this one offer me the opportunity to learn and grow, which is essential. Being a successful consultant does not only involve substantive knowledge and technical skills, but also "soft skills," such as relationship building, listening, communication and leadership. This combination allows a consultant to more efficiently and thoroughly achieve his or her clients' goals.

People from many industry backgrounds and in various stages of their career consider becoming consultants. Young professionals unable to find a suitable position within an organization think of consulting as a possible way to go. Other individuals who have spent many years in one or more positions and would like a change believe consulting is the answer. Still others have retired and are turning to consulting to seek new work opportunities and challenges. These are all legitimate reasons to provide consulting services, but one must thoroughly know and understand what a good consultant can and must do.

This guide takes a comprehensive look at how to make a difference as a consultant. I unpack lessons I've learned from thirty years of consulting in the areas of health, social services, education, employment, justice and human rights. I have conducted extensive research into the dynamics of consulting, and wherever possible, I use examples from my experience. Of course, the confidentiality of my clients is a paramount consideration, so I keep the stories general enough to simply extract the lesson.

I have clients in all levels of government—municipal, provincial and federal. I have consulted with many community groups and organizations in the not-for-profit sector that work with a variety of populations including: prenatal and early years, children and families, youth, single mothers, new immigrants and refugees, seniors, people with physical disabilities and people with mental health challenges. I have worked with Indigenous people, multicultural communities, professional organizations, academics and the general public. I have consulted for hospitals and other healthcare workplaces, social service agencies, educational institutions as well as private sector companies. Much of what I have learned is applicable to any sector or industry.

Part I of this guide addresses how to become a consultant and what it means to help organizations in this capacity. I offer useful information that will help determine if consulting is for you, as well as tips to get you started and steer you on a successful path.

Part II of this guide sets forth the top ten skills essential to becoming a great consultant. These lessons demonstrate how to make a difference as a consultant, confirm you are on the right track and provide food for thought on adjustments you could make to be even more impactful to your clients.

I present the information in this book with humility and with the aim to help make a difference in your work as a consultant.

- Zena Simces

PART 1
Becoming a Consultant

CHAPTER 1
Getting Started

Let's start at the beginning, shall we? What is a consultant? A consultant is a professional who has a certain level of expertise and experience that a group, organization or business requiring external advice or assistance finds valuable and is willing to pay to obtain.

I was full-time in government when I first decided to explore consulting. My boss at the time was moving to an independent government agency responsible for a similar target population. He indicated there were a number of projects that needed to be done and that he would be willing to hire me on a contract basis as a consultant. I had been thinking about a change and, though I was a bit hesitant to leave a full-time position, I had not been there long enough to accumulate any pension, and I knew my client and the sector. So, I took the leap and started with the new agency on a consulting basis. I was happily busy for close to two years when I realized that all the projects my client wanted done were near completion, and I would soon be out of work. I was faced with the daunting task of finding new clients and contracts, which meant I had to start from the beginning and market myself. It takes time to secure projects, get referrals and build relationships with clients. If you are thinking of going into consulting, there are several key lessons I learned from my experience starting out in the field. It is best to find a contract before giving up a full-time job. It is always easier to build from strength. We also need to continuously market ourselves, be visible in our target sectors of work and keep a lookout for new opportunities.

Getting Started – Lessons Learned

- Look for future opportunities while you have a job.

- Develop a marketing plan.
    - o **What** are my marketable skills and experiences?
    - o **Who** am I targeting—which government sector(s), community organization(s), industries or companies?
    - o **How** will I reach my target audience(s)?
    - o **When** do I plan to do this?

- Begin with a list of people you know or those who know people in the sectors you would like to target.

- Focus on a priority niche area as part of your initial marketing strategy.

- Find a longer-term contract to get started, if possible.

- Work with a team of other consultants. Projects are becoming much more complex and often require a variety of skills, so working in a team is a viable option. A good first step is to find a consulting firm that may be interested in your skills. You can also connect with

2

other consultants in the areas you are interested in and see if you can collaborate on projects.

- Seek small projects that you can do on your own, if possible, to begin building your reputation. This necessitates having all the required skills to do the job successfully. If this is your first consulting job, this could be difficult. Seek out projects that relate to the work experience you have.

- Attempt to build repeat business. While working on a project, you may also identify future possibilities for that client. It may not happen right away, but if they are happy with your work, they may reach out to you when more work arises. The consulting industry largely works through repeat business.

- Focus on establishing your credibility. If you are working with a larger consulting company or with other senior consultants, the company may have the credibility. This will help. However, if you are given an assignment or are working on your own, it is more challenging. Many of the attributes of a great consultant outlined in Part II will help establish credibility, but the most important element is to show you can be trusted to do what you said you are going to do in the way you promised. Being able to deliver and demonstrate that you can learn quickly and effectively will go a long way. Credibility also helps to promote repeat business.

- Recognize that at times you may be very busy, while other times you may have much more time to spare.

This is the fluctuating nature of consulting that I found difficult getting accustomed to. I have learned to take advantage of the slow times to market my business, keep abreast of current research and innovations in my areas of interest and to hone in on certain skills and seek out and acquire new skills.

- Ensure you have the technical and substantive skills and knowledge that are required by organizations in your target industry. If you do not have them, you may need to acquire them or secure them on your team.

Technical Skills

a. **Computer skills:** In addition to Microsoft Word, PowerPoint and Excel, graphic design basics and software knowledge are critical as most clients want to see a final report with charts, diagrams, photos, etc.

b. **Statistical analysis:** Developing questionnaires, analyzing data, producing charts and graphs are all essential skills. There is a plethora of statistical analysis software available, and you will need to understand them and choose what best suits the project. For quantitative data, I have used SPSS Statistics, which was developed for the social sciences. Other clients use SAS for advanced analytics, business intelligence, data management and predictive analysis. "R" is a programming language and free software environment for statistical computing and graphics. I have also used QDA Miner to analyze qualitative data from surveys, documents or interviews. There are many others on the market as well.

4

c. **Business knowledge:** Financial and accounting knowledge may be required for billing purposes and, in particular, if you set up your own small company. Be sure to get advice (e.g., from an accountant and lawyer) on the pros and cons of incorporating as a business, especially relating to dealing with business expenses, tax implications and liability concerns. Check with an Insurance Agent if your employer requires you to have Professional Liability Insurance and/or Comprehensive General Liability Insurance.

Certain projects may require you to be able to undertake cost/benefit analysis of programs, services or products to determine if they are being delivered efficiently.

d. **Internet and social media:** These elements are becoming more critical for collecting data, doing online surveys, sharing information, reaching your client's desired target audiences and for marketing yourself. Questions of privacy and confidentiality are increasingly important considerations when using social media. There are many new platforms and programs that can benefit the organization you are working with and your own work. I cover this in more detail in Chapter 5.

e. **Technology skills:** These are broader than computer and social media skills and are fuelled by technological innovations such as artificial intelligence, big data, virtual reality and more. This is the wave of the future and understanding these technologies and being able to access this expertise is critical.

f. Project management skills: Managing all the moving parts of a project is the foundation of a successful consultant, just as methodically managing multiple projects and activities lead to thriving organizations and businesses. Much has been written about project management, and there are many tools and software applications that track progress on projects. I do not have any particular project management tools to recommend but finding one that is simple and meets the needs of your client is the key. Many are complex, and my advice is to keep it simple. Clients are most often looking for a concise summary of work accomplished, progress on future deliverables and outstanding tasks, who is responsible for completing the tasks and the timeline for completion.

Soft Skills

Beyond the technical aspect of an engagement is the interpersonal component. Ensuring all players are satisfied along the journey of the project from initiation to implementation is important. It is not only the interpersonal relationship with the client group, but the working relationship with your team that is critical to facilitate the successful completion of an assignment. Soft skills play a crucial role for ensuring the work moves forward to achieve the desired goals.

Soft skills are therefore essential for consultants. Developing trusting relationships, being a good listener and communicator, having influence and using leadership skills are the main subjects of this guide, and I discuss them in depth in Part II. They are too important to be called "soft" skills and have become the essence of what is required to be a great consultant. In fact, the Business Council of Canada's Skills Survey (2018), which is based on responses from ninety-five of Canada's largest companies, lists soft skills such as collaboration, communication, problem-solving, analytical capabilities and resiliency as top priorities for entry level hires. Companies also valued these soft skills for mid-level employees.

The final and possibly most important consideration is "know thyself." Knowing your strengths and weaknesses is important. We all struggle with self-awareness, but effective consultants recognize their biases and how to address them. They are natural self-starters and strive for excellence in all that they do, so they are aware of their blind spots and work to improve in areas they are weak.

At the start of my career, I was quite impatient and thought I knew more than my clients, so I wanted to direct them. As I matured and gained more experience, I recognized I had to be much more patient, really hear what the client was saying and not be so quick in always trying to find a solution. Recently, I found myself becoming impatient with the clients who were much younger than me and who I felt lacked experience. It takes a great deal of self-awareness and control to be patient, non-judgemental and to guide clients to the best solution for them and their stakeholders.

In summary, start your consulting path when you are in a position of strength and ensure you have a marketing plan. Consider the technical and soft skills you have and what you may need to enhance or acquire. Finally, know your strengths and weaknesses, and "know thyself."

CHAPTER 2
Responding to a Request for Proposal

Most consulting contracts require the candidate to prepare a proposal. This could be in response to a request by a client to submit a proposal or as a response to a formal Request for Proposal (RFP) process. Many government departments and industries are now approaching consultants from a "Qualified List of Consultants". Getting your name added to such a list requires responding to a Request for Qualification and being accepted.

Key Features of A Request for Proposal

Be prepared to write many proposals to compete for consulting contracts or to submit for approval before you commence a project. While the requirements, both content and format, of requests for proposals may vary, in most situations, the following topic areas will need to be addressed:

1. **Understand the project:** Demonstrate you understand what the organization is requesting. Ensure that you

address the client's desired work product and ultimate goals of the project.

2. **Demonstrate experience and expertise:** RFPs often ask the applicant to identify very specific examples of work and skills related to the needs of the project. Think about all your qualifications and expertise, select and elaborate on the particular skills required by the project. If you do not have all of the necessary skills or experience, it is best to partner with one or more other consultants and become part of a team that possess all the requirements.

3. **Provide an overall action plan:** It is a good idea to specify an overview of what you plan to do, why and how you intend to achieve the desired results. Collaboration with the client is essential. State clearly how you plan to keep your client(s) involved throughout the project. This means engagement in every stage of the process. Clients do not want surprises. They want to feel they are part of the process. A detailed, step-by-step outline of the activities to be undertaken can be provided in a work plan (see below).

4. **Clarify data/information collection:** Spell out what data you need to collect, your sources of information and how you plan to collect this information. This is an area where you can be creative to enable your response to stand apart from others. For example, you might suggest a scan of other similar organizations, businesses, programs, services, products or policies as well as competitors in local or broader jurisdictions. You

might suggest a combination of different methodologies including interviews with a wide range of stakeholders, focus groups, town hall meetings, round tables or public forums as well as electronic or mail-in surveys. You could identify the types of questions you will be posing and the need to collect both qualitative as well as quantitative data. Be as specific as you can without losing the focus of the client's desired outcomes. Providing a sample of how the data will be presented to the client may be beneficial. Data presentation techniques or data visualization can impress your client.

I recall one incident in particular where my team indicated in the proposal that we would not only scan the literature and other jurisdictions for similar programs and provide a description of them, but we would undertake key stakeholder interviews and analyze the pros and cons of all of these programs and present strategies for the future. We were not successful in our bid, so we requested a debrief meeting with the client to understand where we did not measure up. We were told that the client felt we proposed providing much more information then they wanted at this point and that we might lose focus on the main purpose of the project. They wanted a documented description of the programs and then they would decide which programs were to be analyzed further in a second phase, if needed.

There are a couple of key take-aways here. If you are going to offer more than what is requested, ensure you clearly demonstrate you are meeting the client's requirements. If you are not successful with your proposal, request a debrief meeting. This can be useful when preparing subsequent proposals for this client and more generally for other intiatives.

5. **Construct a detailed work plan:** Provide a detailed work plan that includes an outline of the activities you plan to undertake, specific timelines (if possible), what your deliverables are, and the anticipated outcomes of each deliverable. This could be outlined step by step, in stages or in phases of work. The challenge is to provide sufficient detail to demonstrate to the client how you plan to carry out the work but not too much detail. I have lost a number of bids because I provided too much information and the client disagreed with some of the specifics. The trick is to find the correct balance.

6. **Identify how you will report/recommend:** Establish what you plan to cover in your report and/or recommendations. Determine if your client would like to see short- or long-term recommendations or strategies and whether they prefer options or alternatives; this opens a discussion about choices.

7. **Establish the time frame:** Specify a realistic overall timeline. Many projects I have been involved in have gone on much longer than anticipated (with no extra budget). Timelines need to be realistic not only for you and the client, but they also need to consider the availability of your information sources and others you are relying upon to assist in the project.

8. **Create a budget:** Present a realistic budget. At times, you know the amount available and you try to fit your proposal into that budget. This can be dangerous because there is often more that needs to be done, but it is easy to ignore those extras in order to comply with the client's budgetary requirements. I often "low-balled" on contracts early in my career thinking it would lead to greater success in securing them. If you are starting off your career and want to establish your reputation, you may be more inclined to put in a lower bid, recognizing that you will spend much more time and energy than reflected in the budget. In general, this is not good practice. I have been burned many times and had to do a lot more work and put in great deal more time than the budget accommodated.

If you miscalculate, it is difficult and uncomfortable to go back to the client after the budget has been approved and the work is underway. In particular, take the following into account:

   i. How much time might be spent administering the project, organizing meetings, preparing status reports, fielding unscheduled communications, preparing invoices? It is important to include an administrative or project management fee.

   ii. How much time might be required for revisions, rewrites or redoing work following client input?

   iii. Include a contingency amount in the budget. I have had a number of clients that once they see what you have produced, they realize that they want something done differently, would like more information, or would like the information presented in a different format. All this takes time and cannot be predicted when we initially begin a project. Professionals in other industries, such as building contractors, include contingency fees, and this is applicable in other sectors as well.

In summary, while clients may request different formats for responding to a proposal, it is always beneficial that you: demonstrate your understanding of the project; illustrate relevant experience and skills; provide an overall plan as well as a detailed work plan; clarify how data is to be collected and analyzed; and specify a realistic time frame and budget. Think of creative but realistic ways to propel your response to a proposal into the foreground in this highly competitive environment.

PART II
Making a Difference: Being a Great Consultant

Over the years, I have heard and received advice about the characteristics of good consultants. They need to be flexible, yet persistent and disciplined, confident, but open to learning, creative and innovative. While these features are important, Part II outlines the top ten characteristics that contribute to being a great consultant based on my experiences and research.

CHAPTER 3
Building Trusting Relationships

If you don't believe in the messenger, you won't believe in the message.

- *James M. Kouzes & Barry Z. Posner*

Consulting is all about relationship building. It is often who we know and our relationship with that person that lands us the work in the first place. Relationships also assist in obtaining repeat business from clients. Solid connections with our clients also help smooth the way to a successful project. As a consultant, we do not have to like or be liked by everyone we work with, however, we do need to establish credibility and trust, which is very different from likeability. People need to buy into the relationship before they buy into the solutions presented.

Trusting relationships with our team members are crucial. Over the years, I have partnered extensively with one special colleague. While our styles of work are very different and we often hold divergent views on significant issues, we recognize and respect each other's strengths and weaknesses. We have established a trusting relationship that has led to many successful bids and completed projects.

Relationship skills are the most difficult to master yet the most important. One of my clients asked me to develop a strategic and operational plan for the delivery of specified municipal services. The client hired a new staff member to manage this project and the consultant team. The first step was to meet with the client and the new project manager to understand what their goals were and what deliverables they expected. I developed a comprehensive work plan that was reviewed by the client and the project manager. The project entailed extensive consultation with staff in various departments, with service providers, consumers of the service and the general public. At each stage, we consulted with the project manager and provided summary reports to keep her involved. However, we soon realized that her boss, our client, had a different perspective, and he questioned the findings we identified. It meant additional meetings and clarifications with the client and the project manager to ensure there was consensus on what was needed and how to proceed.

Upon reflection, I realized I had not taken the time to truly understand the perspectives of the client because I thought that the project manager was reflecting them. While attempting to develop a relationship with the project manager, I had neglected to ensure the client felt comfortable and trusted our work. We developed an acceptable strategic and operational plan in the end, but it required additional consultations with the client and with groups the client had not initially identified. It also meant many more iterations of the final documented strategy to ensure we met the needs of the client and the project manager. This project took a great deal more time than estimated (with no additional funding) largely because I had not securely established a trusting relationship with the ultimate client.

This example shows the importance of taking the time to know your clients' perspectives and values. It is beneficial to discover more about them personally, their work history in the organization and industry and in other positions and jobs they have held. Let them get to know something about you personally in addition to your previous projects and work experiences. While you don't need to share too much personal information, making a personal connection is essential in building a trusting working relationship.

When I have undertaken evaluations of programs or services, there is often an underlying fear held by staff and managers that the program or service might be eliminated and they may lose their jobs. It is critical to gain the trust of all stakeholders, ensuring they have a clear understanding of the purpose of the evaluation to improve efficiency and effectiveness and that they are engaged and participate in every stage of the evaluation.

Trust is a critical component of building a relationship. The client needs to feel they can trust you, that you understand their needs and those of their organization, that you have the knowledge and skills required to carry out the work, and that you can deliver. Trust means consistently doing what you said you were going to do and in the way you indicated you would. Most significantly, the client needs to see and believe that you are transparent, sincere, respectful, and have their best interests in mind. It is important to show you are committed to go that "extra mile" with them. You need to ensure that you honour your clients' confidentiality so they feel free to speak their minds. Clients need to believe they can rely upon you because reliability enhances the trusting relationship. You also need to show that your care. If clients refer you to others, then you can feel confident you have been successful with them.

I am a baby boomer, and I have begun to notice that many of the managers and people overseeing the projects and the consultants I am working with are "Gen Xers" or millennials. (As an aside, many baby boomers are also going into consulting, which makes the competition tougher.) It is important to understand the different characteristics and values of these generational groups.[1] If the consultant and the client are part of different generational groups, it could lead to more difficulty in establishing trusting relationships. Although this is somewhat of a generalization, I have found that the work ethic between baby boomers (who are thought to be workaholics), Generation X (who are thought to be more balanced) and millennials (who are thought to be ambitious, and focused on their own goals) can be very different. Also, the value given to different sources of information may vary. Perceptions each generation has of the experience of the other generations tends to fluctuate. Baby boomers often believe they have the experience and have lived through it, while they feel millennials lack experience and insight. Generally, millennials believe the baby boomers are not as innovative or informed about new technologies and environmental issues. These differences can be challenging in developing trusting relationships, if we do not recognize and

---

[1] https://www.kasasa.com/articles/generations/gen-x-gen-y-gen-z (Accessed October 2020)

consider them, and focus on the positives that each person can contribute.

Building a trusting relationship takes time and patience. It takes what is referred to as "emotional intelligence" where you are not only aware of your own emotions, but you also have empathy and understanding of others and the ability to connect with them. Emotional intelligence is a key predictor of professional success and personal excellence. According to Bradberry and Greaves (2009) in their book *Emotional Intelligence 2.0*, there are four emotional intelligence skills that pair up under two primary competencies:

1. "Personal Competence" is made up of self-awareness and self-management, meaning "Your ability to stay aware of your emotions and manage your behaviour and tendencies."

2. "Social Competence" is made up of social awareness and relationship management, meaning "Your ability to understand other people's moods, behaviour and motives in order to improve the quality of your relationships."

In addition to emotional intelligence, a great consultant also requires cultural intelligence or cultural sensitivity, where we respect and relate well with others regardless of race, culture, language, age, gender, sexual orientation, religion or political beliefs.

As my consulting career has progressed and my daughters have grown and become professionals, they have taught me a few important lessons that are applicable to building trusting relationships. I once heard one of my daughters (who happens to be a psychiatrist) tell my granddaughter, "You may not always like everyone, but you need to be kind to everyone and that will help you develop the relationship you need with them." My other daughter (who happens to be a lawyer) taught me not to jump to conclusions too quickly but to weigh the facts and recognize there are always different opinions and ways to view an issue. These elements need to be respected if we want to establish trust.

A trusting relationship promotes repeat business. From a repeat client's perspective, you are already seen as reliable. Repeat business in the consulting industry helps with job security, which is often a concern. Most of my work has been with repeat clients. A track record of success helps us with new client opportunities and provides a source of effective references when bidding for new work.

The COVID-19 pandemic of 2020 taught us many important lessons about trust in times of uncertainty. We have learned we must trust the expert health professionals and have faith that our community members will wear masks, wash their hands regularly and keep their distance for all of us to be safe. We must rely on employers to ensure the health and safety of their employees and have confidence that restaurants will follow all the safety precautions. During this time, Alison Grenier, the head of culture and research at Great Place to Work® Canada, wrote an article in *The Globe and Mail* (April 2020) that outlines what she calls "Trust Rules," which are the "universal path to trust." These are important lessons for consultants:

1. "Trust First": Be the first to trust; don't wait for others.

2. "Live with integrity": Don't compromise your values. If you feel something is not right, then it most likely isn't.

3. "Keep your promises": Don't break any promises. It's better to say you cannot do something than apologize later for not doing it.

4. "Respect the whole person": Show interest in people and respect them as individuals.

5. "Give straight answers": It's not just what you actually say that counts, but it is also what you omit. The information you omit appears like lying and impacts trust.

6. "Treat everyone fairly": Show respect and that you value equity and diversity.

7. "Show your appreciation": Be sincere and show appreciation at the appropriate times.

KEY TIPS ON BUILDING TRUSTING RELATIONSHIPS:

- Create a safe, equitable space so people feel they can trust you and others at the table. This means everyone voicing ideas without fear, sharing power and learning from each other. There are always power differentials in any organization or group, and we need to recognize that everyone's perspective is valuable. An important role for the consultant is to assist our clients in recognizing the value of their team's perspectives.

- Focus on the person, not just the issues. Ensure the clients feel that you care. They need to feel valued and respected in a genuine way.

- It is okay to show some vulnerability. In fact, it takes courage to show vulnerability, and it takes strength to redirect to find a better solution. This can contribute to greater confidence between you and your client.

- Believe that the people you are working with have the ability to resolve a situation and can get their heads around complex issues. This does not mean "managing your client" but rather tapping into the strengths of the clients or stakeholders and seeing them as important assets.

- Ensure clients know the work will remain confidential until they want it released.

- No alarms, no surprises. Clients do not like being caught "off guard." It is essential that you keep them fully informed along the journey of the project. The well-known expression "Nothing about us without us" is critical to achieving and maintaining trust.

- Build a hub of project-related documents and/or information you can easily share with the client.

- Continually provide and update project progress reports, presentations, etc.

•••

In summary, take the time to know your clients and for them to know you. This creates a safe and foundational environment for the honest and open exchange of ideas. Demonstrating that we genuinely value and respect our clients and that we care about them and their project helps establish trust. Creating a trusting relationship is the first and foremost goal in client relations, and it is an essential skill to being a great consultant.

CHAPTER 4
Understanding Organizational Culture

Organizational culture eats strategy for breakfast, lunch and dinner, so don't leave it unattended.

- Torben Rick

We must know our clients and understand the environment we are working in, but most of all, we must comprehend the culture of any organization we walk into as a consultant. Every organization or workplace has a personality or "culture." Employees have a way of doing things that define how an organization runs. Culture is composed of people but can take on a life of its own. It is more than just the context. Culture includes how people behave, the values, beliefs, customs, written and unwritten rules, the modus operandi (how the organization carries out its business) and, finally, the look and feel of the organization. All of these contribute to the unique organizational culture.

Charles A. O'Reilly, a professor of management at Stanford Graduate School of Business, and his colleagues (2014) define culture as a social control system that drives certain kinds of behaviour. They examined a variety of industries (e.g., Ford Motor Company, Hewlett-Packard, Amazon, to name a few) and found corporate cultures that emphasize adaptability generally produce "revenue growth, market and book value, 'most admired' ratings, employee satisfaction, and stock analysts' recommendations. Adaptive cultures encourage risk-taking, have a willingness to experiment, are supportive of innovation and are faster to make decisions and execute them." The essential mechanism, O'Reilly says, "is alignment of culture with strategy."

Peter Drucker, an Austrian-born American management consultant, educator and author, famously said, "Culture eats strategy for breakfast." Torben Rick (2020), a business consultant in the European Union (EU) with expertise in developing and driving business improvement and change management, more recently wrote, "Organizational culture eats strategy for breakfast, lunch and dinner, so don't leave it unattended. There is a powerful triumvirate in corporate transformations – Strategy, Capabilities and Culture. All three need to be designed together, aligned and enabling of each other to create true organizational transformation."

I consulted with a major fundraising organization that had used particular methods of fundraising for decades. I had done my homework in researching successful fundraising practices in other jurisdictions and developed a number of proposals on how my client could adopt new methods to great success. The organization and its leadership were not receptive to these new, innovative methods even though they were proven strategies elsewhere, when the players/leaders/managers changed over time or when the current methods were not achieving the desired fundraising goals. There was such a strong culture in the organization that supported particular and entrenched methods of fundraising, and there was no appetite for change. Leadership always felt we needed to work harder with the methods we had. There was a fear of change built into the culture of the organization and a belief that the organization's method of fundraising was the right one for them.

My solution was to understand this deeply rooted fear. I brought in senior executives from organizations in other jurisdictions to present their successful fundraising methods to my client's leadership team. Then I identified several champions within the organization who were more receptive to change. In addition, I was able to pilot a couple of different fundraising methods on a small scale. These strategies all helped to engage senior management and employees to be more receptive to other potential fundraising options.

If you see yourself as a catalyst of change, then when you work with an organization or make any recommendations you need to understand the organization and be conscious of whether what you are doing fits into its unique culture, and know when it is appropriate to challenge the cultural norm to create change.

Amelia Chan is the founder and principal consultant of Higher Options Consulting Services and a human resources professional. She believes that the value of the human resources professionals lies in their ability to serve as a culture catalyst (2017). She identifies five fundamentals for fostering positive workplace culture: "Curiosity, Communication, Credibility, Commitment and Agility." I have consistently used these key strategies to assist my clients in promoting a positive culture. Curiosity helps in seeking out the positives and negatives about the workplace culture both for us as consultants and for our clients to more fully appreciate their organization's culture. Promoting open and honest communication at all levels of the organization contributes to a positive culture. Credibility is a key factor for establishing trust, and staff at all levels of the organization need to believe their managers and senior leadership are credible and can be trusted. Commitment to the work and willingness to go beyond what is being asked facilitates a positive culture. Agility is a key factor enabling all players in the organization to be open, flexible and adaptable to changing circumstances to foster positive workplace culture.

• •

KEY TIPS TO UNDERSTANDING ORGANIZATIONAL CULTURE:

- Pay attention to the culture of the organization or workplace and tread carefully. Identify where it is helpful to be supportive of the existing culture and implement approaches to build on it. For example, knowing whether the culture of the organization is collaborative or competitive can help shape the appropriate strategies.

- Assess whether a change in culture is needed. If so, work with leaders of the organization to help them understand what may be required without causing them to feel threatened or overwhelmed. More leaders are beginning to recognize organizational culture as an enabler of organizational success.

- Recognize where the other levels of the organization or employees of an industry are coming from and what will help them feel more secure. Build on their strengths and capabilities.

- Implement an engagement survey. This is one way to gauge the pulse of the culture and the motivation and commitment of staff at all levels of the organization. More informally, it helps to listen to people's conversations and how comfortable they feel to raise issues. You might consider asking people at all levels of the organization such questions as:

  o   How do you feel about going to work?

  o   What makes this organization or workplace tick?

  o   What makes this organization unique?

• •

In summary, be aware of culture, understand it and work with it when you are proposing recommendations for organizational change. Support your clients in understanding the culture of their organization as this will enhance their success in making decisions, executing them and creating positive and profound changes.

CHAPTER 5
Being a Good Listener and Communicator

Listen not to confirm what you believe to be true,
but to explore what else is true.

- Peter Drucker

Listening and communication are crucial skills for effective leaders, and the same is true for great consultants. Listening is part of being able to clearly communicate what we heard.

My team and I were the secretariat for a large inter-disciplinary Leadership Table involving provincial and municipal government departments, not-for-profit community groups, professional organizations, educational institutions and corporate representatives. This Leadership Table identified six task groups to address diverse aspects of the development of a provincial plan to improve the health and well-being of citizens in a province. The aim was to compile the findings and recommendations of the task groups and present the results to the Leadership Table for decision-making. We would then produce a final report that conveyed the consensus of all the players. While this entailed careful listening skills and the ability to analyze and synthesize the information to identify key issues, there were also several other key strategies employed:

- Going back to committee members to ensure what was recorded reflected their recollection of the discussions.

- Skillfully and accurately framing and clearly communicating this information to the Leadership Table for decision-making.

- Highlighting the critical issues that required decisions and providing sufficient background information to enable an informed decision.

- Accurately and concisely documenting the final recommendation. This step required several iterations to ensure the results we documented reflected what the group agreed upon.

Listening

You know you are listening when you understand and can synthesize what the client has said. It never ceases to amaze me that people have such different perspectives and interpretations of what transpired at a meeting and what was agreed to or not agreed to. There have been quite a few incidents when I left a meeting with clients with the understanding that I could go ahead to pursue a particular course of action only to find out later that it was not what they had in mind at all. Listening carefully before you speak helps us communicate more clearly what we hear. Listening before we recommend helps us gain better insights and solutions for our clients.

Listening is the key to diplomacy. The former U.S. ambassador to Canada, Bruce Heyman (2014-2017), co-authored a book with his wife, Vicki Heyman, called *The Art of Diplomacy* (2019) where they indicated, "Diplomacy is about listening and taking the time to understand another perspective before promoting your own views."

Dr. Ablert Mehrabian's 7-38-55% Rule (1971) indicates words, tone of voice and body language account for 7%, 38% and 55 % of personal communication respectively. While this equation was derived from experiments dealing with communications of feelings and attitudes, it is a good reminder that non-verbal cues such as tone of voice, and body language including gestures, facial expression, demeanour, stance, etc. are very powerful in conveying messages. As a consultant, it is important to complement our words during personal communications, presentations or public speaking with the right tone and the appropriate body language. This helps us transmit our messages more clearly and effectively.

Clear Communication

A key complaint I have heard over the years, regardless of the type of work being undertaken, is the lack of communication— or the lack of clear communication—about what is going on and why and how it impacts people at different levels of the organization. If we do not communicate clearly, people tend to make up their own view of reality or their own version of what is going on. This can result in problems.

Listening carefully helps you confirm what is being said but also contributes to exploring what has not been said. Often what is not said may be just as relevant—or more relevant—than what is said. When I detect this, I often use the strategy of posing a question for the entire group or directing it to participants that I observe may be holding back their opinions. I may ask for clarification or if anyone feels they have not had the opportunity to share their views before moving on to another topic. My aim is to lay the groundwork for open and honest communication.

Understanding and communicating what successes look like for our clients are also useful strategies. If we have multiple clients on a project, it is even more important to ensure each can communicate what success means to them. To reach a common understanding, it is helpful to summarize the results of a discussion before we move forward. To cement this, I provide a written summary of decisions and then elicit further feedback.

An additional strategy that has helped me over the years is to determine what the purpose of the communication is before I engage in it. What is the intent of the message? Is it to:

- Inform (i.e., provide clear information as background)?

- Tell a story to gain the interest of the client?

- Ask a specific question I want answered?

- Find a strategic path towards a decision?

Giving this some thought and preparation enhances the effectiveness of our communication. Engaging in clear, open and honest communication with our clients throughout the journey of the project builds greater support and trust, and contributes to overall success.

"Elevator Pitch"

For effective communication, it is essential to distill the key messages down to the salient points. When we are presenting information, it is helpful to think about it as an "elevator pitch." How will I make it stand out? If we cannot explain the main point of what we want to say in two minutes, we need to work on it a bit more. When doing presentations, this "elevator pitch" is valuable to either securing the work or explaining the results of our work. There are two essential components of a successful pitch:

1. Personal touch: It is helpful to personalize, that is, to find a way to connect with our audience (or client) to enable them to identify with us or with the situation. Basically, can they trust me and feel safe with me?

2. Competence: We need to illustrate we have the skills to get the work done or that what we have done is based on evidence, competence and experience.

We want to positively influence how they perceive us and what we are offering.

Audience

When communicating, we must give careful consideration to who our audiences are and to adjust the message to connect to what is important to them. As suggested, while we may need to appeal to people on an intellectual basis, we must not neglect the need to appeal to their humanity as well. Finally, we need to be personable; coming across as authoritative or too vague or "wishy washy" does not help our cause. The aim is to get the attention of our audience in the most effective way.

When communication is respectful, empathetic and centred on individuals, it helps create a safe environment that shows care and supports collaboration and problem-solving.

Framing

A further aspect of communication is the concept of framing. This means presenting an issue in a way that might gain the most support from our clients. For example, if I indicate a product or service will be rejected by 10 out of 100 people, this can be seen as somewhat negative. However, if I frame it as 90 out of 100 people will use the product or service, it creates a more positive outlook. Whenever we are presenting an issue, understanding the attitudes and beliefs of the audience receiving it will help frame the problem. The University of Kansas developed a "Community Tool Box"[2] that I have found useful for guidance on framing and reframing problems and issues.

Digital Communication and Social Media

The way we communicate virtually in today's business world and into the future is critical. For example, our emails can communicate a great deal about our intentions. Am I being curt or vague? Does it sound as if I lack empathy, patience, clarity or

---

[2] https://ctb.ku.edu/en/table-of-contents/advocacy/encouragement-education/reframe-the-debate/main_(Accessed October 2020)

caring? When sending an email, aim to state your main point or ask in the first sentence or two. We have a tendency to skim emails, and the receiver may miss the main points. When using digital technology such as Zoom, Skype, Facebook Live, team collaboration software or other platforms for communicating and holding meetings or presentations, first and foremost, ensure that the technology is working and that you know how to work it. Listening carefully and clearly communicating are just as siginficant when using social media platforms. Remember we are being watched—sometimes more closely—so gestures and facial expressions are even more critical.

Many individuals and organizations are using Twitter, Facebook, Instagram, LinkedIn and other platforms more extensively to communicate information to their networks. As a consultant, these platforms are useful for networking and to market ourselves, our companies, services and products. As you probably have seen from those in the public eye, short and curt tweets can sometimes be misunderstood and cause trouble. Issues of privacy and potential rapid spread of misinformation are growing concerns. Having a firm handle on the functions and etiquette of these platforms and ensuring our messages are relevant and appropriate should be top of mind.

Reporting

When presenting a proposal, findings or recommendations, my key advice is to ensure you are able to condense the information and extract what is critical for decision-making. Make your messages really stand out so the recipient can understand them, remember them and be excited to act upon them. What I have found to be most useful is ensuring that the recommendations are in plain language, begin with action-oriented words and include only one action. It is most confusing when a recommendation contains different and sometimes conflicting messages. If you do not have the skills yourself or on your team, I suggest engaging a graphic designer to format your report, since visual effects have a huge impact.

• •

KEY TIPS ON BEING A GOOD LISTENER AND COMMUNICATOR:

- Listen first and speak second. Think before you talk.

- Summarize and repeat back conclusions or paraphrase what the speaker said as the meeting progresses. At the conclusion of the meeting ensure everyone is on the same page.

- Actively listen to everyone's story and help the group appreciate each other's stories and value the different perspectives and opinions.

- Show genuine empathy, compassion and caring when listening.

- Do not intervene or interject unless you feel it is relevant to the client and could contribute to addressing the issue at hand.

- Volunteer to take the minutes of a session so you have a record in writing that your client and other stakeholders can review and provide feedback.

- Send an email or call to clarify an issue when you are uncertain what your client had in mind.

- Be familiar with what you should and should not do if you are chairing a meeting. Preparation is essential. Online meetings are becoming the norm so, while all the same principles apply, take care to ensure you are prepared and that one person is guiding the process or discussion and one person speaks at a time. There are options on the online platforms to divide up into smaller groups and then come back to a plenary session. This may be a helpful process.

- Monitor your tone closely both when speaking in-person and on social media.

- Avoid what might seem like orders or judgements (e.g., *You should,* or *You should not; I would,* or *I would not;* or *It is obvious that XYZ*).

- Allow participants time to think or assess a situation themselves.

- Ask open-ended questions (as opposed to yes/no questions) to get at the heart of the issue. Ask **Who**, **What**, **When** and **How** questions. For example: Who is involved? What would you like to accomplish? What do you envision would be a good outcome? When would you like the specific tasks or project completed? How would you like to address the situation at hand?

- Think carefully about how you can make your point stand out. Explain it precisely, carefully and relate it to what the client wants.

- Do not force your views or opinions but ensure that points made are understood. As a consultant, you make suggestions and work with the client to come to a decision. We are not there to enforce our own viewpoint.

- Ensure there is some direction for the next step at the end of each meeting.

- Confirm with clients that their expectations have been met, and work to meet them if they haven't been.

• •

In summary, while all of these tips may seem simple and just common sense, trust me, we can get into a great deal of difficulty if we do not listen carefully and then ensure we communicate clearly and precisely. Listening carefully before we speak helps us communicate more clearly what we heard. Listening before we recommend helps us gain better insights and solutions for our clients. Always keep open lines of communication and encourage exchanges of ideas. Develop a coordinated approach to communications. This could entail developing your own communications plan with your client that includes regular updates to all concerned. It may also entail assisting your client to develop both an *internal* communications plan with specific mechanisms to keep the organization informed and engaged and an *external* communications plan to reach out and keep stakeholders, partners and others informed.

CHAPTER 6
Upholding Ethical Standards

We look for three things when we hire people.
We look for intelligence, we look for initiative or
energy and we look for integrity. And if they don't
have the latter, the first two will kill you...

- Warren Buffet

"Of course!" you may say, "as a consultant I need to uphold ethical standards." But what does that mean and whose standards are we upholding? You may be in a situation where your client asks you do something that may be a conflict with your own values. There may be a time when your client requests you to explore a certain issue/problem and they already know the answer they want. They would like you to confirm their conclusions, but your findings are contrary to their desires. What do you do?

I was once asked to determine if a program should remain with one particular agency or if responsibility should be moved to another organization. I soon came to realize that the client had already decided that they wanted to move the program, and they needed a justification. As I was working on this project and interviewing stakeholders, it became evident this change would not be the best outcome for all the partners involved. I prepared a preliminary report and indicated to the client that the findings were pointing to the program remaining where it was. The client was trying to steer me in a different direction that was contrary to the findings, and it became an ethical issue. I could not in all fairness come up with the conclusion the client wanted, so I had to walk away from the project, leaving most of the budget behind. It was a question of my integrity. This may not always be so easy to do.

To uphold ethical standards, we first need to know who we are and what we believe in. We need to think about what principles of behaviour and work we value. I strongly believe that integrity is paramount. Integrity means being honest, sincere, having high standards of behaviour and being transparent. Above all, we need to be transparent in all our interactions. Transparency with our clients is strength.

Further, keeping client confidentiality is crucial. Ethical consultants do not discuss any aspect of their work with anyone. This may seem obvious, but it is critical. Principled consultants never gossip about the people they are consulting for and, of course, never about any members of their working team.

Humility is another important attribute for a consultant. While it is expected of us to be experts and behave with confidence, we need to do so with kindness and humility. This is sometimes difficult to achieve, but being humble can cultivate respect and show you are an authentic person. Humility helps us be less wrapped up in our own ambitions and appreciate the diversity of perspectives and opinions. It also contributes to building trusting relationships, which I have already indicated is critical to being a great consultant.

As a member of a consulting team, we need to understand the views and values of our team members. If they differ from ours, it is important to discuss them openly and honestly. Often, differences of opinion are a matter of degree and can be worked out. If they cannot, it is worth considering whether this is the right project or team for you. The vital factor is to avoid letting differences build into resentment and bad feelings.

I have often heard it said that "managers do things right" and "leaders do the right thing". I believe a consultant needs to do both of these things. This will contribute to good judgement and decision-making.

When I think about ethical standards, it brings to mind the issue of unconscious biases. It is important to become more aware of our unconscious biases and to find ways to mitigate them. I have often heard consultants say that we did not get a contract even though we were just as qualified (or more) because we were an all-female team or they were looking for people younger, more like-minded consultants. Well, perhaps the client did prefer another team because of some unconscious bias. When we are doing our work as consultants, we need to be very aware of our own unconscious biases. Do we tend to agree with a client because they are similar to us culturally or have a similar personality? Do we tend to agree with a particular solution presented by others because it confirms our own opinion? Do we make assumptions about certain groups because of prevailing stereotypes?

This is a tricky area. I have found it is sometimes helpful to write down assumptions that may colour our opinions. We need to seek out and welcome the perspectives and insights brought by those with different experiences from our own. These steps can at least make us aware of our biases and perhaps be more accepting of diverse opinions.

My parents (who were in the grocery business) shaped me as a person and as a consultant. Their motto was to treat people the way I want to be treated.

• •

KEY TIPS ON UPHOLDING ETHICAL STANDARDS:

- Understand what your key values are, what you may be willing to bend on and what your bottom line is.

- Be true to your principles. Be open and authentic about who you are and what you believe in, both personally and professionally.

- Avoid even the perception of a conflict of interest. Appearance of a conflict of interest is as significant as a real conflict of interest. Your work can be immediately discredited if there is any perceived conflict of interest.

- Assess whether the client is open to a range of conclusions and options before you bid for a project or accept the work.

- Evaluate whether your values match with what you perceive to be your client's values. If you're not sure, be transparent and ask for clarification. This may not be a project for you if there are substantive differences that cannot be reconciled.

- Be conscious of your biases.

- Conduct yourself with humility and integrity in all situations.

• •

In summary, remember "honesty is the best policy." Do not try to spin things or put challenges in a better light than they are. Our clients and the people we work with can often see through this, and we risk losing their trust. We build trust by being honest. Know who you are and what principles, values and standards you hold dear. Integrity and honesty are paramount to being a great consultant.

CHAPTER 7
Being a Catalyst for Change

It's about being a catalyst—changing minds by removing roadblocks and barriers that keep people from taking action.

- Jonah Berger

Our success as consultants depends on how well we understand, embrace and be a catalyst for change. Sometimes we may need to change the views of our clients to reach a particular outcome. We may be asked to change the way an organization is functioning or investigate the way a company does business. Any project we undertake will most likely require some type of change. Our clients may be requesting this change and may be ready for it, which is great. However, I have found in many circumstances that the client is not prepared. He or she may have been mandated to undertake a certain change in the organization and may not agree with or be ready for it. Maybe the staff is not in favour. It is not sufficient to simply know the modifications that are required, but we need to understand how ready everyone, at all levels of the organization, is to make a change in order to develop our approach.

I once worked with a client who asked me to complete a service delivery review that would entail major changes in the way the organization delivered its service to its target population. The project entailed a review of the current service delivery, the processes and procedures, and an outline of what was working well and what the issues were. I also undertook a review of other jurisdictions that provided similar services.

The client had a vision of some of the changes required but recognized that many of the staff, who had been with the organization for numerous years, were reluctant to make any changes, and they had very different opinions on what work should be done and how to do it. The client wanted assistance not just in identifying what needed to be modified but also help with bringing staff on board to accept and implement the new procedures. One of the key strategies I used was to consult with all the staff and engage them in the review process. Some staff believed change was not required at all because what they were doing and how they were doing it was just fine. Some staff felt they did not have the time to implement different processes, while others felt that it was not in their job description and they were not being paid to carry out these new responsibilities. Further, others did not believe they had the appropriate skills.

What became evident was that the staff needed to be involved in designing the specific details, as well as participating in how the new procedures and activities were actually going to be implemented. I prepared an initial draft report that identified options and suggestions made by staff and backed it up with evidence from similar programs in other jurisdictions. Engaging the staff in helping to develop an implementation plan, proposing a pilot and developing a phased-in approach were key strategies I used to gain support. Further, securing several champions among the staff also contributed to moving the implementation plan forward.

Many think that the role of a consultant is to provide advice, but unless our advice is accepted and leads to positive results, it is difficult to conclude that we have succeeded. As consultants, we need to understand the process of change and change management to be able to guide our clients through the steps of the projects—from an understanding of the issue, to an agreement on the possible solutions and finally to how the solutions might actually be implemented. Implementation is a critical aspect of achieving success. We have all seen governments propose new policies or legislation that will change how we do things. Sometimes the implementation process reveals flaws and difficulties that can alter the overall intent, exceed the budget and lead to unintentional consequences.

I often suggest to my clients that not only will we be providing recommendations, but also an implementation plan on how they might successfully implement the recommended changes—not only the *what* but the *who* will be responsible, *how* it could be done and suggested timelines.

William Bridges, a leader in change management, indicated that in order to be able to adapt to change, we need to understand that transitions/changes typically occur in stages, as follows:

- "Ending": This stage marks a conclusion in that we need to let go of the past and accept something is ending.

- "Neutral Zone": In this stage, we need to accept that something is ending but we may not have a clear view of what is about to begin. This calls for encouraging renewal, creativity and innovation.

- "New Beginning": In this stage, we need to accept the challenge of working in a changed environment and recognize that some things may have been lost but also that certain gains have been made.

These stages may provide you with food for thought in your work as a consultant, recognizing that in each stage there may be diverse perspectives and emotions as well as different strategies to address them.

A model of change management that is believed to be suited to address the challenges being faced by business managers and leaders in a complex environment is Appreciative Inquiry. Appreciative Inquiry (Cooperrider and Whitney, 2005) is a positive approach to change that discards the problem- and issue-based method and seeks to discover the positive aspects of an organization or business, its assets and strengths, what makes it alert, alive and gives it energy, its "positive core." The four phases of Appreciative Inquiry according to Cooperrider and Whitney are:

1. "Discovery": Engage all stakeholders in identifying strengths and assets.

2. "Dream": Create a clear higher-purpose vision.

3. "Design": Create an ideal organization that emphasizes the "positive core" and the dream that was articulated.

4. "Destiny": Strengthen the system to enable it to sustain positive change.

Appreciative Inquiry asks the members of the organization to define the direction they want to move in and find ways to leverage their strengths to achieve the desired results. A key role of a consultant is to help the organization move through this process.

A different way to look at change that has helped me more recently is well-documented by Jonah Berger in his book *The Catalyst: How to Change Anyone's Mind* (2020). Berger has worked with many different organizations and industries, and he came to the conclusion that you cannot effect change by "pushing harder." He believes that "it's about being a catalyst – changing minds by removing roadblocks and barriers that keep people from taking action." He provides many examples from industry, community initiatives and daily life experiences. The one example that struck me the most was that of hostage negotiators. He relates that these negotiators start by listening, attempting to gain trust, talking through the person's fears, and then easing tensions or pressures the hostage-takers may have so they can look at their situation differently. What they are doing, he says, is trying to identify what is stopping the change and then trying to remove the obstacles that are in the way. Berger presents five barriers to change that he calls the "5 Horsemen of Inertia." His book explains how each hinders change and provides strategies to help remove these roadblocks.

I have briefly summarized these below and illustrated how they have impacted me in my work.

1. **"Reactance"**: If we try to persuade someone to accept some change, they often react against it and push back. Berger suggests we need to first increase understanding, provide information and then a menu of guided choices. In many of the reports and proposals I have prepared over the years, I have provided a number of different strategies for the client to choose from. I have found that the discussion then revolves around the choices—which one would be most viable—and not on one particular recommendation that can be rejected.

2. **"Endowment"**: Berger indicates that when we are endowed to something, it means we are attached to it. Once we become attached to it, we value it and stick to the status quo. It is easy to stay with what we know and have, and we feel it is less costly than changing. Catalysts, Berger says, highlight how much people are losing by sticking to the status quo and doing nothing. He contends that "seeing how much time or money is being lost is more motivating than seeing how much could have been gained." Berger talks about easing endowment—not just making people comfortable with new things but helping them let go of the old things. I have used this strategy to help clients understand what they might lose if they do not make certain changes.

3. **"Distance"**: Berger shows that when people are provided with information, they weigh it based on their belief system and values. If it fits into their "zone

of acceptance," they will agree with it. If the ideas fall into their "zone of rejection," they tend to disagree with it. So how can you move the distance into their zone of acceptance? Berger suggests there are three ways to mitigate distance:

a. **"Find the movable middle"**: Target messages in different ways to different people and find those with a "wider zone of acceptance" (e.g., the undecided in a political voting arena). When I have facilitated sessions with diverse audiences with the aim of helping them agree to a certain strategy, it has been helpful to identify participants whose positions are closest to what I am trying to achieve. I provide an opportunity for them to speak, and encourage their engagement. They often help the group move closer to the change being sought.

b. **"Ask for less"**: Berger indicates that a small ask may be more amenable, and people will go along with it because it is likely to be in their "zone of acceptance." The next time you ask for more, it may be easier to gain their approval. A strategy I have employed in working with many clients is to divide the work into smaller chunks—individual steps or phases—and gain support for each phase as I go along instead of trying to go for the big ask initially.

c. **"Switch the field to find an unsticking point"**: This entails finding where there is already

52

some common ground and building on it. Berger suggests that when people recognize they share similar experiences they can relate to each other better. I have used this strategy often. When working with different community organizations at the same table or facilitating a session with diverse participants, having them share their stories and seeing if others have similar stories or experiences can lead to identifying common ground that can be used to move forward.

4. **"Uncertainty":** Berger indicates that if a person has to choose between a certain good thing and an uncertain but potentially better thing, they most often pick the certain thing. The riskier choice has to be a lot better for people to take the risk because people are generally risk-averse. Change most often involves a degree of uncertainty. The more uncertainty there is, the less people are willing to accept the change. Berger says, "Uncertainly acts like a pause button... stopping action and freezing things where they are." He indicates that to address uncertainly, one of the key strategies is "Trialability." This refers to making things easier to try, which lowers uncertainty and, in turn, makes people more amenable to do something new, use a new product or change their mind about something. Berger gives many examples such as: free shipping for online shopping that encourages more people to buy the product; test driving a car to help you decide which one to buy; renting a place before buying; or tasting

different flavours of ice cream at an ice cream parlour. These experiences all enable people to try something before they need to commit. I have often suggested that clients try a new process or product on a pilot basis for a specified time period to see what stakeholders think before going forward with full implementation. This most often leads to adoption and also to suggestions for improving the process or product before committing to it.

5. **"Corroborating Evidence":** Berger contends, "If multiple sources say or do something, it's harder not to listen, because now there's corroborating evidence... reinforcement." He also says, "Multiple sources also add credibility and legitimacy." Providing corroborating evidence is something that, as a consultant, we do to enhance the credibility of the data and findings. Berger stresses that *who* the sources are is important to consider. Some sources may be more impactful than others. Sources who are dealing with the same or similar issues that your organization is dealing with tend to provide stronger corroborating evidence or proof. While similarity is important, the sources need to be independent and diverse. Diversity adds additional value, and the evidence is not seen as redundant. Many of the projects I have undertaken have included a review of similar services, processes or products provided by similar organizations or industries in other jurisdictions, or a review of the literature on promising or best practices. These types of activities help to provide

important evidence and a more objective perspective to strengthen the recommended change.

Berger goes further to say that *when* the evidence is provided is critical. Concentrating the evidence at a particular time tends to be more helpful than spreading it out, although it depends on what you are trying to change. If it is something that is not a strongly-held attitude and where only a little proof is needed to change someone's mind, you can spread out the evidence. (Berger refers to this as a "pebble with a sprinkler approach.") However, if it's a strongly-held view, concentrating the evidence tends to have more impact. (Berger refers to this as a "boulder," and this needs a "firehose approach.") I have found that it is important to pay attention to when you provide the evidence to ensure your client and decision-makers are receptive to it.

The big lesson I learned during the COVID-19 pandemic of 2020 is that we need to be flexible and adapt to change within our personal lives as well as professionally. The concept I kept hearing during this time is "pivot."

- Can you pivot your approach to the program to incorporate social distancing?

- Can you pivot the way streets and parking lots are being used to create more space for people?

- Can you pivot your business from sewing clothing to sewing masks?

- Can you pivot your production of cars to make special plexiglass or other equipment needed?

Being able to pivot means being flexible enough to discover and create an opportunity to change and adapt to the evolving situation. This is a critical skill now and for the future of consulting.

••

KEY TIPS ON BEING A CATALYST FOR CHANGE:

- Understand the change required and the impact it can have on the client and organization.

- Recognize that flexibility and agility are critical for addressing change.

- Identify what the drivers of change are—external factors such as economic, environmental, demographics, etc., but also internal drivers and personal factors.

- Remain focused on the overall goal or vision. Be open to changing course, if required, both in terms of what needs to be delivered and the time frame, but do not lose momentum.

- Ensure that the changes you recommend are feasible and can be implemented.

- Develop an implementation plan that helps move your client from what needs to be done to how it could be implemented. An implementation plan to accompany your final report is a value-added benefit and a critical aspect of good change management.

• •

In summary, if you want your suggestions and recommendations to be accepted more often, you need to understand the barriers that hinder your clients from moving forward. Being a catalyst for change by providing advice and support to enable your clients to accept, engage and implement desired changes is what great consultancy is about.

CHAPTER 8
Focusing on the Big Picture

*Big picture thinkers broaden their outlook by
striving to learn from any experience. They don't
rest on their successes, they learn from them.*

- John C. Maxwell

Great consultants see the big picture as well as the details.
So often, clients will get caught in the details of a project and
lose sight of what they want to achieve overall. Sometimes
consultants get caught up in the personalities, and it's easy to
blame challenging situations on difficult clients. I have often
been upset because clients change their minds so often or
they are too slow in responding and negatively impact project
timelines.

I was involved in a project where the clients (from three
different agencies) kept changing their minds on what they
wanted done and how they wanted it to be done. My challenge
was to determine if they were altering the main goal of the
project, and if so, why and how? Or was the big picture the

same but they were identifying varied or conflicting means to reaching the vision? Once I was able to determine that the big picture remained the same for them, I could then identify they were expressing conflicting strategies to reach their desired outcomes. I organized several meetings with the clients and their representatives to address commonalities and differences in the approaches they were espousing and whether we could reach consensus. In many situations, as in this one, the terminology and some of the details differed but there was a great deal of common ground and a win-win situation for all three clients to enable the project to move forward.

The key to success is to keep our focus on the big picture. Are we still on track for the main goal? Have we departed too significantly from the route we agreed to? I keep reminding myself and my clients about the overall goals and objectives while addressing the details of the projects. It is important to connect the details and the steps along the way to the big picture and to bring your client along the path.

A big picture perspective requires consultants to have vision and insight into future needs, strategies and innovations. We need to focus more broadly on different situations and experiences. Consider the drivers that will impact the future such as changing demographics, technology, economics, and changing consumer and social/health priorities. How might these factors impact the project and outcomes? Finding the answers requires curiosity and, at times, thinking outside the box, being courageous to reach innovative solutions, and being able to think critically and analytically. The big picture perspective requires the ability to analyze the flow of information from many sources, identify the pros and cons of a situation and remain open-minded to the best possible solutions.

A focus on the big picture means understanding the environment in which we are working. I mine all the information I can about my client, the organization, their competitors and other similar projects. Some projects require an environmental or jurisdictional scan to identify what is going on elsewhere to shed light on the work at hand. I pay close attention to economic factors that may impact the project, including any competitors. The political context is crucial as well. Consider the small "p" politics within the company or organization and the larger political environment that may be impacting the initiative.

When evaluating a program or service, understanding the big picture is critical to how we plan our strategy. It is important to know whether the overall intent is to increase quality, improve on delivery, enhance the functioning of the organization, or to downsize or eliminate the program.

There are two key factors that make it difficult in our technological society to focus on the big picture: information overload and the appeal of storytelling. With the vast amount of information available quickly from different sources as well as conflicting information, sifting through it and presenting what is most relevant for decision-making is a challenge. The ability to decipher what information is relevant at what point in time to facilitate the momentum of the project is a crucial attribute of a successful consultant. Identifying what information may be significant in the short-term without falling into the trap of being short-sighted is a skill. Presenting too much information can elevate anxiety and impair decision-making as can presenting information that is too far into the future.

Our society is more and more interested in the story itself rather than the facts. Misinformation, different interpretations of information and storytelling can blur the facts. Storytelling has become a very popular method to transmit information. For some cultures, storytelling is the key method of sharing information from one generation to another and for preservation of their culture. Storytelling is compelling and can be very effective. My caution is to ensure that you convey truth through the stories and that the stories are true to the facts. Again, not an easy task; being conscious of this is a first step in helping to keep focussed on the big picture.

• •

KEY TIPS ON FOCUSING ON THE BIG PICTURE:

- Focus on what your client wants to achieve overall.

- Continuously ask "So what?" This helps to focus on priorities and ensure what you are doing is relevant.

- Remain flexible and adaptable because, at times, the big picture and overall goals may change. However, recognize the shift and ensure your clients are in agreement with the change. Develop your project plan in a way that builds in this needed flexibility.

- Retain purpose and perspective on the overall goal through effective communication.

- Be conscious of information overload and storytelling that does not tell or reflect the true situation and the big picture of what needs to be achieved.

- Keep an eye on the details that comprise the desired outcome. Those details need to be aligned and in harmony with the goals and objectives.

- Increase your chances of success with the right balance between big picture and attention to detail.

• •

In summary, consultants need to lead with intention, focussing on what is important and how best to get the work done in the current and future volatile, uncertain and complex times. Clients need to walk away feeling inspired and confident that the job will be done efficiently and effectively and that we have not lost sight of the big picture.

CHAPTER 9
Considering Collective Impact

Co-creating the future and building collective impact efforts is a path that can only be walked 'at the speed of trust'. It takes time. It takes skills. It takes the creation of safe spaces. It needs to be rooted in our current reality. Perhaps most importantly, it takes our personal commitment.

- Liz Weaver

In promoting change within diverse groups—be it an organization, an industry, a neighbourhood, or an entire city— it is helpful to be familiar with the framework of collective impact. There is a growing literature on collective impact, what it means, why it is important and how to go about achieving it. Collective impact is an approach that moves from seeking single isolated solutions to working on a larger scale for greater impact through collaborations and cross-sector coalitions and partnerships.

When I was working on a project to address the issue of how to enhance the wellness in neighbourhoods and within an entire city, the organizations I was working with had come together previously to address this overall issue, but with little success. It became evident that to ensure the diverse agencies representing different sectors could effect change in their city this time, certain conditions for working together needed to be met. This is where my knowledge of the framework of collective action was very beneficial.

I initially worked with each organization separately, gaining their trust, and then brought the partners together along with their managers and staff. We met many times to enhance their understanding of each other, build relationships and identify a common vision. This eventually led to selecting specific initiatives or activities that each partner could complete on their own as well as what they might be able to do together to achieve this vision. We set processes in place to enhance information sharing and ongoing communications including committees, meetings, documentation, updates, etc. We developed an overall strategic plan and agreed upon many actions. However, the actual implementation and impact of the actions did not go as far as we intended. We were missing two other ingredients that would have enhanced the collective impact: a shared system of measuring and reporting on results, and the infrastructure (e.g., co-ordination, staff and funding) to support the ongoing actions.

Kania (a managing director) and Kramer (co-founder and managing director) of FSG Management Consulting firm identified five conditions that need to be fulfilled to move from isolated impact, where individuals or groups operate independently and advancement is achieved through the work of each organization individually, to what they have coined as "collective impact" (2010). The alignment of these five conditions can lead to powerful results. They are:

- **"Agreement on a common agenda"** where all participants have a shared vision of the change needed or common understanding of the problem/issue and an overall joint approach to solving it.

- **"Development of a shared measurement system"** where there is an agreement on the ways success is measured and reported. Each organization/group may be collecting its own information, but there is agreement on what is to be collected, and measuring results is based on criteria everyone agrees to.

- **"Implementing mutually reinforcing activities"** means that each organization or group can continue to carry out its own specific set of activities but there is a co-ordination of their differentiated activities based on overall plan of action everyone agrees to.

- **"Building continuous communication"** does not only refer to sharing of information but establishing a common vocabulary (which takes time) so the diverse groups understand each other. It means Identifying clear, ongoing communication strategies that include face-to-face interaction.

- **"Establishing a backbone structure"** dedicated to managing the entire initiative, keeping it operational and sustainable is paramount. Without resources to ensure this type of co-ordination and infrastructure support, it is difficult to achieve collective impact in the long-term.

It is worth noting that this original collective impact framework has more recently been revisited by Mark Cabaj (associate of the Tamarack Institute) and Liz Weaver (co-CEO of the Tamarack Institute). While they are committed to the basic structure of collective impact, their work in communities to generate change has led them to move from "common agenda to community aspiration, from shared measurement to strategic learning, from mutually reinforcing activities to high leverage activities, from continuous communication to inclusive community engagement and from backbone structure to containers of change" (2016). This revised framework is worth further study for those consultants who are engaging diverse sets of stakeholders to co-create solutions to complex organizational and industrial challenges, or those working with large community social, health or environmental transformations to co-design better outcomes.

• •

KEY TIPS ON CONSIDERING COLLECTIVE IMPACT:

- Recognize that the collective impact approach can result in greater success than the isolated impact approach that dominates many initiatives.

- Understand that the collective impact approach may be useful for large-scale initiatives, not just in the social sector but in a variety of other sectors with diverse interest groups.

- Educate clients on the collective impact approach and secure their buy-in as a first step.

- Take your time and be patient. Achieving collective impact requires building trust among the stakeholders.

- The Tamarack Institute (www.tamarackcommunity. ca) has many examples of successful initiatives where the collective impact framework has been used.

• •

In summary, in working with large-scale change and diverse sectors, it is worth exploring a collective impact framework that allows you to move beyond the single impact of an initiative in the short-term to strive for broader impact in the long-term. It is not sufficient to simply engage the diverse stakeholders in reaching common ground and undertaking complementary and supportive actions. Sharing a common database and having continuous communication goes a long way to achieving greater impact. However, I have found that this cannot be sustained unless there is solid infrastructure with designated responsibility, co-ordination and funding to keep the momentum going toward continuous improvement.

CHAPTER 10
Being an Influencer

Often we don't realize that our attitude toward something has been influenced by the number of times we have been exposed to it in the past.

- Robert B. Cialdini

It is always crucial that we base our work and recommendations on evidence so clients can make evidence-based decisions. However, we also need to persuade and influence our clients to accept our recommendations. Persuading people that they actually have the power to change things is a desirable skill of a great consultant.

One of my projects entailed reviewing a program's intake process for determining eligibility for and acceptance into the program. The staff responsible had been following the same procedures for many years, felt it was the best way to address the situation and did not see the need to change anything. First of all, my team researched similar programs across the country and documented the evidence for different ways of undertaking the intake process. Providing this evidence was not sufficient. We had to find ways to persuade the staff that this would make their work more efficient and would be more effective in the long run. We convened meetings with staff in small groups and worked with them to consider different scenarios and how we could handle the processes. We reviewed the options with the staff a number of times to enhance their comfort level with the proposals. We talked about trying different procedures on a small scale to assess them and then coming back to a larger group to report on what they had tried and what could work. Once we had some staff on board, they helped to influence others. We held several meetings of the larger group of staff and gradually built a model everyone was willing to try. This was a slow process because the element of persuasion played a significant role.

A number of the reports I have written ended up sitting on a shelf and nothing became of them. I've learned that if I want to make a difference and ensure my recommendations are implemented, I need to provide my clients with solid evidence but also offer suggestions on how to influence decision-makers to take action. Are there financial barriers that could be addressed by presenting potential new funding sources? Are there partnerships or endorsements that would help enhance the political acceptability of the recommendations?

To enhance the influence I have with my clients, I have found a number of helpful strategies. At times, I have shown clients what they might be losing if they don't move ahead, rather than what they might gain. This can work with certain clients.

Most importantly, I always keep my clients abreast of every aspect of the project as it moves along. As mentioned previously, the activities you are carrying out and the recommendations you propose should never be a surprise to them. They need to feel they are a part of the process and the solution. We do not own the work we are doing, and we need to be clear that we are doing it with them. It is the client who owns it, whereas our role is to guide them to ensure they take ownership. The clearest sign of successful influence is when we plant an idea and the client picks up on it, grows it and identifies it as his/her own. This is real influence. Some psychology is involved here.

Robert Cialdini, professor emeritus of psychology and marketing at Arizona State University and best known for his work on persuasion and marketing, identified six principles of influence that are briefly summarized below (2007).

- "Reciprocity": Doing something for others helps to get others to do something for you.

- "Consistency": Sticking to our word and doing what we said we would do.

- "Social Proof": Getting buy-in from a key person in the organization who takes action will more likely result in others following along.

- "Liking": People like those who like them. Finding common ground or providing genuine praise may help achieve this.

- "Authority": If you are perceived as an expert in an area, others will more likely defer to you.

- "Scarcity": People value what is scarce, so finding an exclusive strategy is beneficial.

Cialdini later proposed a seventh principle, which he called the "Unity Principle" (2016). This is where the "influencer and influencee can identify with each other." Cialdini believes that mastering these principles of influence will enable one to maximize their abilities of persuasion. However, he also emphasizes that these principles should be used "from a place of good." These principles can be useful to you as a consultant, but don't abuse them. They can easily be used to manipulate and control. Your influence needs to be authentic, genuine and lead others to the best decisions for themselves and everyone else.

I would like to share with you one particular method of consultation in which the aim is to influence diverse individuals to reach common ground on critical issues that may impact them. You may have heard of "deliberative dialogue." There are different models of deliberative dialogue, and much has been written about it. Julia Guzman clarifies that deliberative dialogue is a method of engaging people with diverse perspectives and competing interests to come together in small groups to weigh ideas and options about a specific issue (1999). Deliberative dialogue provides an opportunity to take a deep dive into an issue and listen and hear other viewpoints once people have had the opportunity to confront an issue over an extended period of time. The dialogue begins with personal stories about the issue, then listening to other opinions. Over time, participants begin to see the value of other perspectives and most often reach common ground.

My team and I used a form of deliberative dialogue called "guided deliberative dialogue" to engage citizens in discussions about the quality of the healthcare system. The aim was to determine if participants could be influenced to move from their particular personal experience to a broader community understanding and to solutions that would be equally good for all. Each group was designed to have nine to twelve participants with representatives from three different stakeholder groups: healthcare providers; frequent users of the healthcare system within the past two years; and infrequent users who had limited contact or no contact with healthcare practitioners for the past two years. We prepared questions to guide the conversation. Each of these groups, at the start, had very different perspectives on the quality of healthcare. While we tested different types of dialogue models including in-person and teleconference, the one that consisted of four two-hour face-to-face conversations once a week over four weeks had the strongest results. There was a measurable impact on participants' views. They came to share a positive understanding of the healthcare system, were able to discuss differences openly, and they began to problem-solve, seek trade-off and reach common ground.

• •

KEY TIPS ON BEING AN INFLUENCER:

- Do not push your own agenda.

- Be persistent when appropriate but not too persistent if you see the client is resistant.

- Provide good information and evidence to support the decisions you wish to influence.

- Bring people along by knowing where they are coming from, as well as when and how to bring up controversial issues.

- Address barriers to acceptance.

- Seek opportunities to find common ground.

- Find champions to influence others.

• •

In summary, to make a difference and ensure your recommendations are implemented, you need to work with your clients to provide them with relevant, solid evidence. You also need to influence them to accept the recommended course of action and, if required, help them influence the decision-makers. Take the time to address barriers and seek common ground to influence your clients toward positive outcomes.

CHAPTER 11
Managing Your Work/ Life Balance

Manage your energy, not your time.

- Tony Schwartz and Catherine McCarthy

Another valuable lesson I have learned is the significance of time. Time is a finite commodity, and how we use and manage our time is important. Working as a consultant may not be a 9-5 work day, and when we have a deadline to meet, we may be working many long hours. We can be very busy or not so busy. Not having sufficient time to do the work or having too much free time can cause stress. How do we know when to take on new projects and when we are already overloaded with what we have?

I have found that projects and demands from clients are becoming increasingly complex. There may be an expectation (whether I put it on myself or it is expected from the client or the team) to put in longer hours. This can backfire and we can become exhausted, burned out and even sick, and the project can become depleted rather than enriched.

When you are overloaded with work, how do you manage? Some people like to do the easy things first to get them done before tackling the more difficult ones. Others advise to start with the difficult ones to get them done so you feel relieved. I have found it depends on my mood, and both methods can work. What is critical is to clearly outline what needs to be done and set a schedule to do it. Even if I have to revise my schedule, writing it down has been the best strategy for me to ensure I use my time efficiently.

Also, getting the work done on time is important for our clients. Sometimes being too quick to submit a deliverable can lead to clients having too much time to review and change their mind. This may lead to more rewrites than I planned for or doing the work over again. We need to be thoughtful and take enough time to ensure we cover what the project outline dictates.

Much of the work consultants do can be done from home, but this requires good management of our time and a certain amount of discipline. I find it helpful to get ready as if I am going out for a meeting or to a work site. Creating positive morning habits to get started each day is important, including getting dressed, eating breakfast, exercising (if you build this into your morning routine), answering important emails and then getting started on work. Ensure you have the right tools to collaborate such as conferencing capabilities and online platforms. Ensure you have a secure environment to work in and that the work you produce is secured and backed up.

The 2020 COVID-19 pandemic has forced more people to work from home, and there are differing experiences. It is surprising to hear how some people have adjusted quite well while others have indicated a dislike for it. The demands on families, with parents working and children at home, have increased stress levels. Juggling your work and personal life and finding a balance is not easy at the best of times, and COVID-19 has magnified the stress for many. It has, however, taught me that it is so important to create a plan and a schedule that sets out time for myself, my work and my family.

Schartz and McCarthy of the Energy Project in New York City profess that you need to "manage your energy, not your time." (2017). This holds true for consultants when we feel overloaded or when we are stressed because we do not have sufficient work. We need to recharge ourselves and take responsibility to renew what Schartz and McCarthy say are the four dimensions of personal energy: "physical, emotional, mental and spiritual". Addressing these areas can go a long way toward achieving a greater sense of alignment within our lives and our work. For me, activities such as jogging, Pilates and playing tennis keep me not only physically active but also sane. My emotional and mental energy is further derived from talking to my children, grandchildren and friends on a regular basis. My spiritual needs are met by reading books that have nothing to do with my work. Each of us has to find how we can address these dimensions and this, of course, will be different for everyone. Care in addressing these areas will render a better work/life balance so we can make a greater difference as consultants.

• •

KEY TIPS ON MANAGING YOUR TIME:

- Ensure a balance between work and leisure. Find time for yourself and your family.

- Create a plan and schedule to manage your time.

- Divide roles and responsibilities to manage time if you are working with others.

- Devote time to look for new business even when you feel you need to focus on the current project you are working on. This will help keep work in the pipeline.

• •

In summary, develop a plan that helps you recharge your energy and efficiency. This will create a positive work/ life balance and contribute to your effectiveness as a consultant.

CHAPTER 12
Using Leadership Skills

Leadership is about making others better as a result of your presence and making sure the impact lasts in your absence.

- Sheryl Sandberg

Before I became a consultant, I held a number of senior management positions in government and the not-for-profit sector. I came to the realization that a good leader needs to be able to assess divergent opinions and conflicting evidence and render a good decision that can make the difference. It is about making the right decision at the right time. Leaders also must be willing to act to implement the decision.

When I became a consultant, I recognized that not only did I need to assess complex situations and make good decisions, but my role was to help my clients lead and make the best decisions to achieve their desired outcomes for lasting impact. It is important to understand your clients' leadership style and work with it. I have had many clients who are controlling. They wish to direct you on what to do and how to do it and are constantly interfering in the small details of the project. In these situations, I keep the client completely informed at every stage of the process with written and verbal reports. I brief the client on the different perspectives and ideas that are circulating among the staff and external stakeholders. I present different options and scenarios to discuss with the client at each critical point in the project, to enable them to take the lead in choosing how to proceed. This is an intensive iterative process taking time and patience but helps your client feel in control while enabling the project to advance.

Some of my clients have been reluctant to take a lead role and have difficulty making decisions. In these cases, my team work with the staff, gaining their confidence and getting them on board to make changes. In addition, I have often volunteered to prepare presentations that the client could use with senior leadership. I ensured the client had answers to all the critical questions that may arise. These strategies help the client take ownership and achieve the desired results.

It is also important to understand the leadership style you have as a consultant in order to enhance your own effectiveness. Within my own team, I had a tendency to be more controlling, always checking on the work that the team was doing and requesting to review their work. I had to learn to be more adaptable, flexible and follow the lead of my teammates. However, in situations where the project could be jeopardized, I needed to use influence and leadership skills to ensure the work was done in a timely and effective manner.

I have learned many lessons from the vast literature on leadership skills, the different leadership styles and from the gurus who write about leadership. Much of what I have learned about leadership is very applicable to being a great consultant.

Carol O'Connor, a consultant with over thirty years teaching leadership and working on five continents for businesses, governments, charities and professional firms, outlined seven simple steps to being a leader (2016). While leadership may not be as simple as she has outlined, her seven steps can be useful. I have extracted key points from her work that are relevant to being a consultant:

1. "Self-awareness" is the single most important leadership quality. Leaders need to examine their behaviour regularly to continue their growth and improve their self-knowledge.

2. "Understanding people's needs and hopes" creates bonds of loyalty and trust. It is also important to know what motivates people.

3. "Communication skills" are often taken for granted but are essential. Also important is the impression a leader makes.

4. "Authority and power" means being confident enough to invite challenges, questions and comments from other people.

5. "Making decisions quickly and implementing them" is important, but this requires identifying priorities and setting goals.

6. "Connecting and linking to bring people together" means we need to be trustworthy and able to build trust among others.

7. "Vision and inspiration" are the most difficult leadership skills to develop, but they yield the greatest reward. Vision opens the way to possibility and invites people to be inspired to create new opportunities.

More recently, Bernard Marr, an international best-selling author, futurist and one of the world's top five business influencers has identified "14 Essential Leadership Skills during the 4th Industrial Revolution" (2019). These are worth noting and could be considered vital skills for consultant's work now and into the future:

- "Active agility" to embrace change.
- "Emotional intelligence" to perceive and understand peoples' emotions.
- "Humble confidence" to encourage others to shine.
- "Accountability" to gain respect of others.
- "Visionary outlook" to see beyond the immediate to long-term solutions.
- "Courage" to face the unknown.
- "Flexibility" to accommodate changing needs.
- "Tech savviness" to understand new technologies of the future.
- "Intuitiveness" to read what is not being said.

- "Collaborative nature" to work alongside the team.
- "Quick learning" to quickly assess complex situations.
- "Cultural intelligence" to appreciate diverse and global perspectives.
- "Authenticity" to build connections and trust.
- "Focus" to maintain attention on what needs to be accomplished.

The leadership literature speaks to many different styles of leadership, some of which may shed further light on key features that are relevant to being a great consultant. The most applicable leadership styles for a consultant to consider are: adaptive (flexible) leadership, situational leadership and transformational leadership.

Gary Yukl, a professor in the management department at the State University of New York at Albany, outlines why flexible/ adaptive leadership is essential and indicates that it involves altering behaviour in appropriate ways as the situation changes (2010). In our current fast-changing environment of globalization, technological advancements, diverse cultural needs, new forms of social networking, and greater focus on the need for sustainability, businesses, organizations and governments require consultants who can understand the context and make decisions and adjustments in response to new information and ongoing flux.

Situational leadership, according to Ken Blanchard, a leadership guru, works on the assumption that the most effective style of leadership changes from situation to situation (1993). To be most effective and successful, a consultant (similar to a leader) must be able to adapt his or her style and approach to diverse circumstances.

Another type of leadership that is currently being highlighted in teaching is called transformational leadership. This is a theory where a leader works with teams to identify needed change, creates a vision to guide the change through inspiration, and executes change in tandem with committed members of a group. The concept was first developed by James MacGregor Burns, a leadership expert and presidential biographer. According to Burns, transformational leadership can be seen when "leaders and followers make each other advance to a higher level of morality and motivation" (2004). As a consultant, being able to inspire others, gain their trust and respect and energize them to achieve higher performance to benefit the organization is a unique skill that can be extremely beneficial.

Edmondson and Harvey identified another form of leadership in their book *Extreme Teaming: Lessons in Complex, Cross Sector Leadership* (2017). They speak to the functions of leadership for extreme teaming, which they define as "cross-sector collaborations." Organizations and companies are increasingly required to work with ideas, skills and people outside of their organizational boundaries to address complex problems and seek solutions. Consultants working in these types of environments need to understand these functions to be able to support them. The four leadership functions for extreme teaming are:

1. "Build an engaging vision": Make values clear and specify challenging targets to reach.

2. "Cultivate psychological safety": Display real caring, which means you care about everyone's perspectives and you see these divergent views as a resource to be leveraged and not as something difficult to manage.

3. "Develop a shared mental model": Find interfaces that will promote discussion and co-ordination as well as "transfer, translation and transformation of knowledge across boundaries."

4. "Empower agile execution": Enable space for project participants to explore, progress and make decisions regarding tasks that fall within their expertise.

It is important to remember that being a good leader also means you know how to follow. That does not mean you follow blindly, but you might need to go into the trenches to fully understand what the organization or industry is doing. As a consultant, this calls for a thorough understanding and appreciation of the workings of the organization at all levels.

Throughout my career as a consultant, I have had to use my leadership skills in almost every project I've undertaken. Along with my team, I have to judge whether I take a leadership role to get the work done effectively and efficiently, or if I can follow the lead of others. With my clients, I have to assess their leadership styles to determine how much of a lead they want to take in the design and implementation of the work. I need to assess whether my clients are prepared to take a lead and what support they require to ensure the recommendations are accepted and implemented. What I have learned is that consulting, like leadership, is all about people. It requires merging relationship skills with sound evidence and having the courage to act for the benefit of all.

· ·

KEY TIPS ON USING LEADERSHIP SKILLS:

A number of critical leadership qualities that can benefit a consultant now and into the future include:

- Adapting to change.
- Knowing how best to deal with ambiguity.
- Providing clarity to situations.
- Acting consistently and competently.
- Being creative and innovative.
- Above all, showing compassion and empathy.

· ·

In summary, the 2020 COVID-19 crisis has shown us that good leaders need to be able to act quickly and consistently while being strategic and courageous. This applies to consultants as well. It is about being able to make difficult choices and the courage to act upon them. It is about leading with purpose and empowering others for lasting impact. Leadership skills permeate every aspect of the role of a great consultant.

SUMMARY THOUGHTS

In summary, to make a difference and be a great consultant, pay attention to the following:

➢ Focus not just on the "problem" but the "people." Great consultants focus on building trusting relationships.

➢ Recognize that it is more important to "get it right" when you are providing advice than "being right."

➢ Show that you not only have the skills, experience and can do the job, but that you care.

➢ Get buy-in and better results by doing the job "with" your clients and not "for" them. A great consultant does not tell their client what to do but shows them how they will do it together.

➢ Be courageous enough to admit you do not know everything. Find the information to address what you do not know. Don't be afraid to ask questions or to ask for clarification.

➢ Take time to analyze your failures. Learn and grow from your mistakes and never give up. You may encounter unforeseen circumstances and negative feedback, but you can learn from every setback to help prevent it from happening again.

➢ Ensure you assess, evaluate and incorporate what you learn to address new challenges. Every encounter is an opportunity for learning. Great consultants never stop learning.

➢ Introduce new creative and innovative insights that may enhance your client's program, organization or business. Seek strengths and assets that can be enhanced.

➢ Strive for excellence and be sincere and trustworthy.

➢ Look for the win-win in all that you do.

➢ Focus on open communication, establishing credibility and commitment.

➢ Be flexible and agile to accept and adapt to change.

➢ Be future-focussed in your work and in your advice, leaving a legacy of strategic change for positive results.

Finally, recognize that the world is moving, and you need to move with it. YOU can have an impact. YOU can make a difference as a great consultant.

SELECTED BIBLIOGRAPHY

Berger, Jonah. *The Catalyst: How to Change Anyone's Mind.* New York: Simon & Schuster, 2020.

Blanchard, K., Zigarmi, C., Nelson, R. B. "Situational Leadership After 25 Years: A Retrospective." *Journal of Leadership and Organizational Studies* Vol.1, No.2 (1993), 21-36.

Bradberry, T., and Greaves, J. *Emotional Intelligence 2.0.* Talent Smart, 2009.

Bridges, W. *Managing Transitions: Making the Most of Change* (3rd ed.). Boston, MA: Da Capo Press, 2009.

Buffet, Warren, (Accessed October 2020) https://www.businessinsider.com/warren-buffett-hire-people-with-integrity-heres-how-to-find-them-9

Burns, J. M. "Transformational Leadership." Langston University. (Accessed October 2020) https://www.langston.edu/sites/default/files/basic-content files/TransformationalLeadership.pdf

Business Council of Canada. "Navigating Change: 2018 Business Council Skill Survey."

Cabaj, M., and Weaver, L. "Collective Impact 3.0: An Evolving Framework for Community Change". *Tamarack Institute, Community Change Series,* 2016. (Accessed October 2020) https://www.tamarackcommunity.ca/library/collective-impact-3.0-an-evolving-framework-for-community-change

Chan, Amelia. "Five Fundamental Traits of a Human Resources Culture Catalyst", *Chartered Professionals Human Resources, British Columbia & Yukon, People Talk – Culture,* Vol.24 No. 4 Winter, 2017.

Cialdini, Robert. *The Psychology of Persuasion.* Collins Business, 2007.

Cooperrider, D. L., and Whitney, D. *Appreciative Inquiry: A Positive Revolution in Change.* Berrett-Koehler Publishers, Inc., 2005.

Drucker, Peter. *Managing the Non-Profit Organization: Principles and Practices.* HarperCollins Publishers, 1990.

Edmondson, A. C., and Harvey, J-F. *Extreme Teaming: Lessons in Complex, Cross Sector Leadership.* Emerald Publishing Limited, 2017.

Grenier, Alsion. "Trust Rules." *The Globe and Mail* (Toronto, Ontario), April 17, 2020.

Guzman, Julia. "SPEAKUP! Engaging Policymakers with Educators and Communities in Deliberative Dialogue," *Insights on Education, Policy, Practice and Research,* Number 9 Southwest

Educational Development Laboratory, October, 1999. (Accessed October 2020 https://sedl.org/policy/insights/n09/1.html

Heyman, B., and Heyman, V. *The Art of Diplomacy: Strengthening the Canada-US Relationship in Times of Uncertainty.* New York: Simon & Schuster, April 2019.

Kania, J., and Kramer, M. "Collective Impact." *Stanford Social Innovation Review,* 2011.

Kouzes, J. M., and Posner, B. Z. *The Leadership Challenges: How to Make Extraordinary Things Happen in Organizations.* Jossey-Bass, 2017.

Marr, Bernard. "14 Essential Leadership Skills During the 4th Industrial Revolution." *Forbes Magazine,* 2019. (Accessed October 2020) https://www.forbes.com/sites/bernardmarr/2019/05/13/15-essential-leadership-skills-during-the-4th-industrial-revolution/#5640401fa3a0.

Maxwell, John, C. *How Successful People Think: Change Your Thinking, Change Your Mind.* Hachette Book Group, 2009.

Mehrabian, Albert. *Silent Message.* Belmont, California: Wadsworth Publishing Company, Inc., 1971.

O'Connor, Carol. *Leadership in a Week: Be a Leader in Seven Simple Steps.* John Murray Learning, 2016.

O'Reilly, Charles, et al. "The Promise and Problems of Organizational Culture: CEO Personality, Culture and Firm Performance." *Journal of Organizational Behaviour,* first published August 2014.

Rick, Torbin. "How Organizational Culture Eats Strategy for Breakfast, Lunch and Dinner." *Supply Chain 24/7.* (Accessed October 2020) https://www.supplychain247.com/article/organizational_culture_eats_strategy_for_breakfast_lunch_and_dinner/legacy_supply_chain_services

Schwartz, T., and McCarthy, C. "Manage Your Energy, Not Your Time." *Harvard Business Review,* October 2007.

Weaver, Liz. "Turf, Trust, Co-Creation & Collective Impact". *Tamarack Institute* 2017. (Accessed October 2020) https://www.tamarackcommunity.ca/library/turf-trust-co-creation-collective-impact

Yukl, G., and Mahsud, R. "Why Flexible and Adaptive Leadership is Essential." *Canadian Psychology Journal: Practice and Research,* Vol.62, No. 2 (2010), 81-93.

ABOUT THE AUTHOR

Zena Simces is a senior consultant for strategic change and president of Zena Simces & Associates, a health and social policy consulting firm. She has over thirty years of experience in the health (population and public health, primary care and mental health), social services, education, justice and employment sectors.

She has a unique combination of expertise in research, program evaluation, strategic planning, policy and program development and organizational change along with a solid background in community consultation/facilitation, community development and engagement, marketing, communications and public/media relations.

Ms. Simces has managed many complex projects working in the public sector (government at all levels—federal, provincial and municipal in the provinces of New Brunswick, Ontario and British Columbia), the not-for-profit and private/business sectors. Zena has facilitated numerous consultation sessions with a wide range of community organizations, professional groups, business communities, academics, diverse cultural groups, First Nations, women, seniors, families, youth, people with mental and physical challenges and the general public.

Her strengths lie in organizational change, community engagement and capacity-building. She has a strong track record of completing projects successfully and has had a profound impact on making a difference.

Manufactured by Amazon.ca
Bolton, ON